ONE SECOND IN HEAVEN

PALMETTO
PUBLISHING

Charleston, SC
www.PalmettoPublishing.com

One Second in Heaven
Copyright © 2022 by Gerard J. De Santis

All rights reserved

No portion of this book may be reproduced, stored in a retrieval system, or transmitted in any form by any means—electronic, mechanical, photocopy, recording, or other—except for brief quotations in printed reviews, without prior permission of the author.

First Edition

Hardcover ISBN: 979-8-8229-0313-5
Paperback ISBN: 979-8-8229-0314-2
eBook ISBN: 979-8-8229-0315-9

The author expresses his thanks to Nicole Marie De Santis and Jay Boyarsky for their helpful editing suggestions.

ONE SECOND IN HEAVEN

Stories of the Afterlife Told by People that Experienced Such and Returned to Life

GERARD J. DE SANTIS

This book is dedicated to all who believe in an afterlife and especially those that lost a loved one and wonder where they may be.

Table of Contents

Chapter 1   1
Celestial Time

Chapter 2   13
Stories of ADE

Chapter 3   41
Expel Damnation

Chapter 4   49
The Devil

Chapter 5   57
Reincarnation

Chapter 6   73
Coins, Feathers, and Scents

Chapter 7   83
Statements of an Afterlife

Chapter 8   97
Provocative Thoughts

About the Author   107

Introduction

The intent of this book is threefold:

1. To present earnest stories of after-death experiences (ADEs) told by people who died and returned to life.
2. To present and challenge certain religious teachings and norms.
3. To present peripheral subjects regarding the hereafter.

As for the first topic, my hope is that their stories will bring a measure of peace and happiness to those who are seeking finality in their understanding of where a loved one who crossed over the line of human life may be now. I too have lost my dearest love, my life partner, my best friend in a wonderful marriage that we shared for fifty-seven years. I know the hurt, thus this undertaking.

In doing the research for this book, I discovered that many stories of near death experience (NDE), or as I prefer ADE, have given me hope and comfort that my loved one is in a good place and that in time we will meet again. I truly hope that this book brings hope, comfort and peace to you as well.

Chapter 1

Celestial Time

CHAPTER 1

I am not a prophet, nor can I predict the future. I am an ordinary person who believes in God and an afterlife and is trying to understand the concept of death and time as it applies there. In doing so, I have developed certain tenets that are of comfort to me. I pray it brings comfort to you too. One such belief is that time in the afterlife is much different than time living humans' experience. It must be so! If it was not, those loved ones that have gone to the afterlife before us could not truly be happy knowing they left their loved ones behind.

Humans are an interesting group. We often use words to describe events without regard to the depth of the meaning of the words we use. An example is the word forever. How long is forever? We all know it means there is no end, but can one truly grasp the time span? In my attempt to do so, I choose to believe that *one second in heaven is equal to a lifetime on earth*. In my mind, this creed satisfies the question of why those in the afterlife do not miss their earthly loved ones. As they bask in the love of God, they do not miss those left behind because they are only gone one second of celestial time. This belief is not without scientific merit. Albert Einstein, in his theory of relativity, postulated that time is relative. In other words, the rate at which time passes depends on your frame of reference. The best way to explain this is with an example. Say there are twin brothers, and one was to travel into outer space at near the speed of light, while the other stayed on earth. If the one who traveled into outer space returned to earth one hundred years in earth time later, he would have aged very little, while his twin would be long dead. The key to this theory is the question when your soul departs your body, does it do so at such a speed as it travels to the afterlife? I believe it does!

In my lifetime, like so many others, I have experienced unusual events. Those events made me stronger in my belief in God and an afterlife. Also, having been raised

CHAPTER 1

a Christian, I believe Jesus is the son of God and that all things are possible through him. You may believe differently. That's your choice!

After Death Experiences (ADEs)

I am interested in and often read stories about the experience of people who died and were brought back to life. The stories they tell of what they experienced while in the death stage have many similar aspects among them. These people often describe going through a long tunnel that has a very bright light at the end of the tunnel, and many believe the love they experience as they near the light is love from God. As I read those stories, it filled me with great hope and happiness that I too will have that experience when I pass from this human form.

One recent story I read was about a woman who was on the operating table in a major city hospital when she expired. She had no heartbeat and no pulse. She was clinically dead! It took the medical personnel quite a few minutes to revive her. Later, in the recovery room, she described to her family what she had experienced while in the death stage. She said she met Jesus, and the love she experienced was so great she did not want to return to her body. She asked Jesus if she could see a loved one who had died some years earlier, but Jesus told her it was not her time, and she must go back to her human form. Stories like this fill me with awe and inspire me to search out more to share with you.

That is my intent and desire, but before we explore some of those events, I have something personal to share with you. Some years back, I underwent a medical procedure. The procedure was to be performed on an outpatient basis. That is, I would enter the hospital in the morning, have the medical procedure performed, and go home in the afternoon. Well, that is not what occurred. Initially all went as expected. Then, after the operation while I was still under sedation, I experienced an out-of-body event

CHAPTER 1

(OBE). It was brief and only lasted several seconds. Like so many others, I found myself looking down at my body as I lay on the hospital gurney in the recovery room. I saw and heard a nurse directing others regarding other patients. "This patient is going home, and this one…" she said, pointing to me on the gurney, "is not!" She then approached me on the gurney and in an urgent tone called my name, "Jerry! Jerry!"

At that point, I was back in my body, but I already knew I was not going home that day. When the doctor who had performed the operation visited me in the hospital room later that same day, he expressed his concern. He told me that during the operation, I had lost a considerable amount of blood, and he had had a very difficult time stopping the bleeding. For quite a while, I was reluctant to tell anyone about the out-of-body experience in fear of being ridiculed. I did some weeks later, however, tell my wife and children.

You see, when I write about OBE, I write based on firsthand experience. As for ADE, I rely on others who experienced it, and their stories are so intriguing.

What did it feel like to have an OBE? In my experience, it seemed like it was just vision. I had no sense of a physical body or feeling of any environmental conditions—just vision and awareness. I would like to believe it was my soul looking back at my body. While in many cases, OBE appears to be the initial stage of ADE, I had no sense that death was imminent, though I may be wrong.

There was another event I experienced that I consider a true miracle. This I did share immediately with my beloved wife and children, and they know what it involved and believed what I told them. I consider the miracle very personal so I will not go into detail about it in this book. However, I will say the miracle occurred immediately after I prayed to God in the name of his son, Jesus. The event took place right in front of me. It was so profound

CHAPTER 1

it strengthened my faith immensely. I have thought very much about that event and wondered why other prayers for other things I prayed for over my lifetime did not have the same immediate result. I finally arrived at the conclusion the reason is that time I prayed for someone else's concern and not my own.

Many people fail to recognize the many blessings in their life, and when they experience rough times, they tend to forget them. Each blessing is a gift from God, and when bad times arrive, they should recall those blessings and not discard them. From my research thus far, I have learned that about 17 percent of people who died and returned to life experienced and remembered meeting God. Their stories are filled with joy and love. So much so they did not want to return to their bodies. While in the death stage, most had no concept of time. Again, time was meaningless or vastly different. *One second in heaven is equal to a lifetime on earth.* I do not have a conclusion as to why the remaining 83 percent who died and returned to life have no memory of their death, nor will I attempt to speculate.

In my research, I discovered there are those who believe NDE/ADE is not proof there is life after human death. In their attempt to debunk the many events people who died and returned to life say they had while in the death stage, they say these experiences are simply a function of their brains coping with death. They cite controlled studies of brain activity as a result of drug inducement. Many of those studies revolve around people who are physically ill and on their deathbeds to begin with. One such study compared several hundred people who said they had had ADEs to thousands of individuals who had been given one or more of many different types of psychoactive drugs. They are determined to prove that God does not exist, and they are sincere in that effort. However, they fail in their attempts! They fail because they have not considered

CHAPTER 1

those who died as a result of instant death by accidents or sudden death. Their stories of what they experienced are so very similar to those who died while undergoing a medical procedure. In their minds, they did not fear they would die because there was no reason for them to believe so. While some of those drugs, such as LSD and methamphetamines, can affect the brain and create illusions of grandness, it does not explain why so many people describe the same aspects to their encounters, such as going through a tunnel toward a brilliant light and the joy of feeling absolute love. Drugs may create an effect of feeling good and other types of illusions in a particular individual, but I don't know of any drug that will impart the same experience of going through the tunnel, seeing the light, and feeling the love in a host of people from many different cultures. That is something the naysayers have not proven as being untrue. Also, I have found no explanation of why people experience OBEs. While in many ADE stories, OBE appears to be the initial stage of death, there are no claims or proof it is. I may be wrong, but I do not believe I was close to death when I experienced my OBE, and yet, to me, it was so very real.

While the intent of this book is to be positive in my presentation of ADEs, I found it necessary in the previous paragraphs to briefly debunk naysayers! Now that I have done so, I will continue to pen happy and true stories of life after death.

CHAPTER 2

STORIES OF ADE

CHAPTER 2

One very inspiring after-death experience that I read was written by Missy M. I paraphrase,

> I died on September 21, 2020. I hovered over my body seeing the work being done by doctors. I traveled into a bright light followed by a tunnel of sorts made with very vivid bright swirling colors. I heard a "music" that greatly resembles a heart chakra vibration. When I arrived "God" manifested as Christ figure—he said we are all one energy connected. Then said my purpose was to go back and spread love and light. As I was returning, I saw my daughter on an airplane she was praying for me to not die, she needed me. I knew what she was wearing, the song in her ear buds, what she was texting—I was in a coma—impossible.

I found this after-death experience to be awe-inspiring. The knowledge one has while in the death stage appears to be boundless.

In another inspiring ADE story, a woman describes her experience after a car accident:

> Then I was surrounded by light so intense I could feel it. It just sort of permeated me. I felt this enormous love and well-being—peace if you will. I had some sense of omniscience or knowing everything. I felt that everything was right as it should be. There was a purpose to everything. I felt knowledge and glimpsed godhood…There was absolute understanding, absolute love, and absolute peace.

To know everything…Wow! What a wonderful thing to experience.

CHAPTER 2

Another interesting near-death experience I read was LaRhonda D.'s:

> I had a tumor on my pituitary gland and had surgery to remove it in November 2019. During that surgery I had multiple strokes, believed to be the result of removing the tumor. The first thing I remember is being in darkness. Not scary, but peaceful. It was as if I were asleep. Then I opened my eyes and surrounding me was a beautiful golden light. I then noticed my hands and saw the light swirling around them. After a few minutes of admiring this beautiful golden glow, I looked ahead of me. I saw in the distance magnificent golden walls. I saw an opening and standing on the inside of the wall was a

beautiful girl around age 10. I immediately knew she was my daughter. While pregnant with my son, he was not the only one, there was a second baby that grew until the end of my first trimester. Standing there was that baby, I knew this by looking at her. No one told me, it was just intuitive. I got excited and started running towards her. I got to the entrance, mere inches from her. She smiled at me and said, "Mommy!" I then came to an abrupt stop. I couldn't move, although I wanted to, more than anything. I felt a hand on my shoulder, I turned around to see who it was. It was a very tall figure, who had a white robe with [a] loose fitted hood. Instead of seeing a face, I saw an incredibly bright light. This light didn't hurt me

CHAPTER 2

to look at, but I couldn't see through it. I believe this was God. He gently turned me around and we walked away. I didn't want to leave but I couldn't resist. My feet moved without me trying. I then entered into the darkness again, and when I opened my eyes again, I was in an empty room except for a bed. This was a hospital bed, and on the bed laid me. I wasn't alone, beside me was what looked like grandfather who passed away 5 years prior. I was excited to see him, but he would not look at the real me, only the body. I felt that if I were back inside of that body, I would be able to be with him again. When I entered into myself, I was alive again. I don't remember much of what happened to me after that because I had a long recovery and was on a ventilator. But I am now well, I have memory problems and am now half blind. But that is seared into my mind, and I will never forget.

Besides the vivid contents of her ADE, what I found so interesting and unlike most other ADEs is the description of physically walking and the feeling of touch on the shoulder.

CHAPTER 2

Another very detailed ADE I read on Facebook was written by Jeremey W. I paraphrase,

> I'm sorry for the long post. I made it as short as possible only leaving out a few details. Seven years ago (Labor Day weekend) I was at home with my wife and both of my kids. At that time, they were 3 and 5 years old. My wife asked me if I would fill up our small swimming pool out in the backyard so that the kids could swim. I walked over to my neighbors to ask if I could use an extra hose. During that time, my phone rang, and I was talking on my phone to a friend as I walked into the house to go out back using our back door to get the pool ready. As I walked in, I remember seeing my kids on the floor both were playing with some toys and my wife was in the kitchen getting breakfast ready. I

was getting confused, even remember saying that to my friend over the phone. Then out of the blue I felt really dizzy and it felt like I was being bear hugged and my head was about to pop off my shoulders. Then, all of a sudden everything went calm, and I saw a bright light off in the distance at which I started toward, but I wasn't walking I was floating. I then saw myself above my body. I was able to see outside and inside my home at the same time. I could see my wife, kneeled down above me doing CPR. Both of my kids were on the couch crying holding each other. I saw a police car and ambulance pulling up in front of my house. I then went back into a realm of where I was traveling again on a path and the light seemed to be much, much brighter. I then saw some

CHAPTER 2

people to whom I never seen before, but it was as if they knew where I was going, and they kindly nodded to greet me and moved over to the side to let me pass by. It was like I knew them forever and I loved them like family. I felt so calm then I was right back to me overlooking my body at which a policeman was doing CPR. Paramedics were pulling different equipment out getting ready to shock my body. There was total panic taking place, yet I couldn't do anything about it. And my wife was frantic, and I could see my body laying there at which time I knew something had happened to me but didn't know what it was. Then I went back into where I was traveling toward the light again and I saw fields of different types of flowers. They were all different colors, beautiful colors I have never seen before on earth. There was also a wheat field that was as far as I could see and one single tree in the middle of it. The wind was blowing the wheat stalks back and forth. Off in the distance I can see a huge wall and it was glowing brighter than anything I ever witness. And there was a gate that was white, and it was in the middle of the wall that was far as I could tell, it went from one end to it looked to be 1500 miles wide and 1500 miles tall. It was enormous. I then saw my dad who past-away years ago and it was like he was driving. And I was laying down in the back seat of what I visualized was a car just (like I remember doing as a child when we would take family trips.) And he looked so young and healthy, and I remember he

CHAPTER 2

looked over at me and rubbed my head and said, "Hang on son we will be there in a minute." Not knowing where we were headed, I just felt safe, the brightness from the light was drawing me closer and it was real comforting as it was drawing me near welcoming me. I was in a valley between two huge mountains, and I remember looking at them and they were both covered in mansions and houses, and they were completely built, and the scripture came to me about God preparing us a home as long as we accept him as our lord and savior etc.... My life flashed before me from being a kid on my mother's breast feeding me to being a teenager and so on and I then heard God's voice speaking to me. I began to worship him although I couldn't see him. His presence was so strong. I began to cry, and he told me this he said, "Child of mine this is not your time to come to heaven because you're not ready yet to sit at the foot of the cross, you have more to do for me for your job is not over." He continued. "There are a lot of people on earth that think they are righteous enough to make their eternal home here in heaven, but they too are lost, and as you go back to your earthly body son. I want you to tell everybody that you come across that Heaven is real and so am I, God your father and my son Jesus Christ, then he ended it by saying you must go back now." And I woke up in a hospital bed confused and not knowing what had happened or why I was there. I thought we were there for my wife because she was standing over me. I asked what we

CHAPTER 2

were doing here? She said it was for me, but I thought she was joking. I couldn't feel no pain then my chest was sore. I was lying in a hospital bed with gown on and an IV etc. The doctors came in and they were all happy as they checked my vitals and I asked what happened and one of the doctors said you have been in a coma for 9 days due to you having cardiac arrest at home. Unlike another cardo vascular arrest, I have ever seen, you are lucky to still be alive. We didn't think you were going to pull through this. My wife said they had brought in paperwork to fill out in case I didn't make it. I fell back asleep. When I came too, I begin to tell my wife what all I remember and what all I witnessed and as I was telling her she began to cry. She then told me there was no way that I could have known that because I was dead during all of it. She's a nurse for over 16 years and said "when she turned me over after I fell face down in our living room floor my face and tongue had already turned purple and I was making that death rattle in my lungs because she could hear it and I had no pulse at all. That she worked on me and kept me until help came. And the paramedics had to shock my body 4 times in the living room before they could put me in the ambulance. Once inside of it then two more times at the hospital. And they had to shock me 3 times while in the helicopter as I was being flown to the trauma center. (That's when I think I saw my dad and him telling me to hang on) during one of those shocks. I ended up pulling through the ordeal. It was a long recovery."

CHAPTER 2

Thus far, of all the ADE stories I read, this was the most detailed description. Surely, he did not dream those events as he was dead. How do you dream you are in heaven when you have no knowledge you are dead? Also, time did not seem to matter, as he was in a coma for nine days.

In my reading about ADE/NDE, I learned about another form of death experience that I found fascinating. It is referred to as *shared near-death experience* (SNDE). SNDE is when other people who are physically near someone who dies also experience the initial phase of the person's passing. One such story was told by Jeff T.:

> It was June 27th, 2019, when I had this shared death experience. I just got back to her room with the Chaplin. He asked if he could say a prayer and he did. He had to leave pretty quickly for some reason. I sat down next to my wife of 34 years and was holding her hand when she began to pant. I

knew at that point she was going to pass. I stood over her with my palms up and begged God to take her gently. I looked down and seen a smile come over her eyes and she tucked her head between her shoulders as if someone was going to tap her head, then she stopped breathing. I saw her come out. It looked like a cylinder type thing. I could see her face at the end of it. She was looking toward her feet and I looked to see what she was looking at and looked back and she was still there. It didn't look like her, but I could only see her profile until she smiled big like she seen someone and took off really fast! I was not in shock or emotional at all. I was hurt a little because she didn't say goodbye. At that moment I felt this unbelievable Love. I feel it was from God himself. It was like I was in a tornado of love. I lost time

CHAPTER 2

somehow because I thought it was 4 pm when asked what time she passed. Since then, she has returned to me several times. Many were just dreams but others were not. There is much more but trying to keep it short. There is definitely life after death. It has changed me so profoundly that I can't wait for my turn. I do not fear death at all. If I knew I was going tomorrow I would celebrate today. I just can't make it happen. I do look forward to it. As should we all.

I cannot think of anything more satisfying than to share your loved one's entry into the afterlife and having the feeling of great love throughout the experience.

I read about shared death experience or, in this case, a shared out-of-body experience in another story. I don't recall the author's name, but it was about a team of firefighters trying to put out a forest fire when they became trapped and as a group experienced OBE. Many of them described the same event: they were above their bodies looking down. They also described seeing their fellow firefighters also looking down at their bodies at the same time. They all survived the ordeal and remember their shared out-of-body experience. The story was quite compelling and made me think if soldiers on the battlefield experiencing the same thing as the firefighters did when, as a group, they may have passed the line of death.

The following information is from an article I read on the web written by Mr. John Blake of CNN. He wrote about a man named William Peters who worked as a volunteer in a hospice where he had a strange encounter with a dying man. The dying man's name was Ron. He was inflicted with stomach cancer. As the story goes, one day, Peters sat down beside Ron's bed. Ron was at that moment semiconscious. Peters said he felt a force jerk his

CHAPTER 2

spirit upward, out of his body. He said he floated above Ron's bedside, looking down at the dying man. Then he glanced next to him to discover Ron floating alongside him, looking at the same scene below.

"He looked at me, and he gave me a happy, contented look as if he was telling me, 'Check this out. Here we are,'" Peters says.

Peters then felt his spirit drop into his body again. The experience was over in a flash. Ron died soon afterward.

Again, more proof of SNDE.

Hopefully as I continue to do research on this subject, I will learn more about such and note it in a future chapter.

On Monday, August 23, 2021, as I arrived home after doing some out-of-house chores, I found a delivered package on my front step. In the package was a book written by Betty J. Eadie titled *Embraced by the Light* that my sister-in-law Nancy had gifted me. I had heard about the book, and I was anxious to read it. As I read through the pages, I found it very interesting, particularly the chapter titled "Embraced by the Light." It described Eadie's ADE in great detail. Like so many others, she vividly experienced going through the tunnel toward the light. The description of what she experienced is so detailed that I am sure anyone who reads this book will also feel like they are embraced by the light. In my mind, it gives more proof of God and life after earthly death.

A woman I know very well told me that after she gave birth to one of her children, she became extremely ill and, in her words, nearly died. With her experience, she said she saw the tunnel with the light in the distance, the same as so many other people described seeing while in the death stage. However, she did not progress into the tunnel but instead found herself back in her body as she lay on the hospital bed. This occurred many years ago. Again, the connection of the tunnel and the light is so prominent.

CHAPTER 2

Another ADE I read about on Facebook is that of a woman who, in her fifties, was ill with a blood disease. As she lay on a hospital bed in the emergency room, she heard a nurse say that her blood pressure had dropped to thirty over zero. At that point, she had only a second of fear, and then everything went black. Then, all of a sudden, she was in a brilliant white light. She described that the light was made up of billions of tiny twinkling lights, like diamonds. The light rushed past her as she also had the experience of traveling into the light at a very rapid speed. She said she was in perfect peace and knew she had died. It didn't matter. She was perfectly OK being dead. She then experienced a life review and, in her words, said she didn't have one bad memory. There were no broken hearts, no insecurities, and no fears. She said there are no words to describe the peace; it was perfect! She was on her way to God! She had no intention of returning back to her body but felt a struggle as the nurses attempted to revive her. She then heard a nurse say, "Open your eyes." She did so but closed them again to get back into the light. However, there was nothing but darkness when she did. She spent several weeks in the hospital.

I found this story very interesting because she knew she had died and wanted to remain in the light. The peace she felt must have been so inviting.

Another Facebook story is about a woman who took an overdose of drugs and died. In death, she met her father who had passed several years before her. She said he was with two other people in white clothes, and her dad took her and showed her this beautiful garden. They then went to an open field that seemed to go on for miles. She could see children playing and running through the grass, they were with a couple of adults. It was the most beautiful field of different colors she had ever seen. Then her dad said to her that it was OK, and it was not her time to be there and that she had things to complete. She did not

CHAPTER 2

want to return to her body, as she felt so peaceful there. She said, "So much love there, but my dad led me back. I woke with doctors and nurses around my bed. My life today is so much different. I have great love for people now. I saw a better place and have more things that I must do while alive."

Because of her ADE and the love she experienced in the afterlife, she is a completely different person today. She now accepts life and is grateful for the experience of death.

There are many stories of people actually seeing the spirit of a loved one leave their earthly body as they crossed from human life to the afterlife. As these people witnessed the event, they expressed the feeling of absolute love. In addition, there are also reports of those who passed sending messages to a living loved one in various ways.

One interesting report was that of a woman whose sister passed, and she desired to receive some sign from her. She was particularly depressed, not having received such, and was deep in thought as she was driving her car to go shopping one afternoon when out of the blue, a car cut in front of her. The car's license plate read, "ANIE-1." Her sister's name was Annie, and she was the only sister she had. In addition, the automobile license plate was on a blue Ford. Blue was her sister's favorite color. Having that experience, it instantly brought great comfort to her.

Another ADE I listened to on YouTube was that of a man named Jim. Jim was raised in Canada and wrote a book about his experience in the afterlife after dying from a rare illness. The story he tells is so emotional, you actually feel and see his emotion as you watch his face while he relates his ADE. Jim said he met guarding angels, and he saw beautiful flowers of different colors. Yes, he also met Jesus! But before he described those events, he was

CHAPTER 2

faced with a monster of sorts that came from a bottomless pit. He said he heard the cries of the condemned coming from inside the beast. He felt that he also was going to be condemned and was saved only after he cried out for God to save him.

What makes this story so remarkable is that he apparently died while out of favor with the Lord and yet was redeemed by calling for God to save him. God's forgiveness is endless.

I have a wonderful niece who recently told me that when she was visiting her mother one day in the hospital, they were having a nice conversation about recipes. It was around the holiday time, and she and her mother (my sister) were talking about holiday baked goods, such as cakes and so on. All of a sudden, her mother looked up, faced the wall, and said, "Dad, what are you doing here?" Her dad (my father) had entered the afterlife many years earlier. When my niece asked her mother if she saw her father, her mother brushed it off. The next day, her mother passed into the afterlife.

From this account, and there are many more like it, it appears a relative comes and helps you in the afterlife journey.

CHAPTER 3

EXPEL DAMNATION

CHAPTER 3

Without a doubt, none of us on this earth will escape the experience of human death. It is an essential part of life. At some time, we will all enter that phase of passing from the human realm to the spiritual hereafter. How we meet that moment depends on our belief that our spiritual being will continue to progress to a better place. To do so well, we must rid ourselves of the fear of death and the notion of damnation. I personally do not believe in a place called hell where your soul is condemned forever in fire and pain. To me, God is love and peace and would not create such a condition. In my thoughts, if you have an undeserving soul when you die, your soul will not earn the joy of an immediate afterlife. I suggest your soul is recycled (reincarnated) until it is right and acceptable for God's eternal afterlife. Death is a soul-cleansing process; the good progress, and the ill-faithed get a do-over. But the soul is not in a fiery place for eternity. God is all about love and peace. He is not a tormentor.

It is interesting to explore where the thought of hell came from. The word itself is derived from an Anglo-Saxon word *hellia* that is used in the King James version of the Bible to enhance the Jewish concept of Gehenna, as the destination for the wicked. The fact is Gehenna is an earthly place, not an afterlife place. It is a valley outside the walls of Jerusalem that was notorious for being the most unholy place on earth, a place where, according to the Old Testament, the ancient Israelites practiced child sacrifice to foreign gods. Thus, Gehenna (hell) is earthly and not a place in the afterlife.

I am sure there will be many folks, including some Bible study evangelists, who will take issue with my statement of no damnation. They will quote scripture as though it is the only truth. While the Bible is a good book and the intent is to bring knowledge to you of God, in some ways, it is a restricted message in that it is portrayed as the only true words, as though God were the author of

CHAPTER 3

the present-day Bible. You must realize that ancient scripture has undergone so many interpretations and language changes, and with each, individual interpreters put their own belief and spin on its meaning. In some cases, the message today may not even be close to the initial meaning. Because of that, as free-thinking people, we must consider that what is written in the Bible today may not actually have the same meaning as it had when it was first recorded. Let me give you an example how that could have happened.

Many years ago, if I recall correctly, there was a game show on television where there were about ten people lined up single file. The first person would read a statement in silence and then whisper into the ear of the next person what they had read. The second person would then whisper into the third person's ear what they had heard from the first person and so on until the last person in line would recite out loud what they had heard. The result was often so different from what the first person had told the second person. Well, consider the complexity of the Bible. Can you really accept that there were not changes in the message? The reason why I bring this to your attention is to say don't be bullied by other humans in what they demand you believe. In the name of God, be true to your belief. God understands.

It is also important to understand that while I take exception to certain writings in the Bible, I believe, overall, it is a very good accounting of the life of Jesus. In support of that belief, there is an organization that has done an exhaustive investigation on the validity of the New Testament. That organization is CrossExamined.org. I suggest to get a full perspective of the New Testament, you read their accounting of it.

An interesting fact is that many people, particularly in America, believe there is a hell. This information was stated in an article I read on the website Tomorrow's

CHAPTER 3

World. It said that the Barna Research Group reported, "While there is no dominant view of hell, two particular perspectives are popular. Four out of ten adults believe that hell is 'a state of eternal separation from God's presence' (39 percent) and one-third (32 percent) say it is 'an actual place of torment and suffering where people's souls go after death.'" As I noted before, I don't believe in hell. Again, God is all about love and forgiveness, not torment! However, I can accept that the absence of God would be hell.

As I continue to do research about after-death experiences, I found very interesting the many questions people have regarding that subject. At first, as I read some of their questions, I wondered if they were serious in asking them, but then I realized, most were and were just seeking answers to assure themselves that their loved ones who crossed over were in a good place. If they got that assurance, it might possibly help them deal with their earthly loss. However, while the questions are directed to those who have experienced ADE, often, answers are given by people who have not had such an experience. Their answers most likely are derived from the point of view of their own belief. The fact is, none of us know until we experience it ourselves. The true answer is in our hearts, in our belief in God and an afterlife. If you truly believe, you already know they are in a good place.

Chapter 4

The Devil

CHAPTER 4

This is a short chapter but a necessary one. The title may seem a bit odd since in the previous chapter I expounded upon the belief that in the hereafter there is no such place called hell. With that being the case, is the devil real, and if so, where does it dwell?

According to the Bible, the devil is known by many names. Lucifer, Mammon, Beelzebub, and Belphegor are some of them. The common aspect between all those names is that they represent evil. Thus, is it possible that the devil and evil are one in the same? There is an old saying: "The devil within!" Does the devil actually exist within the minds of each person?

We all know that humans are capable of doing evil acts. What we don't know is are souls also responsible for those acts? Is the soul influenced by the human, or is the human influenced by the soul? While humans can be evil to the point redemption may not be possible, according to the teachings of many religions, it is the soul that has redemptive qualities. This is a very complex and touchy subject and for sure will stimulate a lot of controversy.

Another facet that makes the devil/evil and where it dwells even more difficult to comprehend is the topic of reincarnation. According to the process of reincarnation, the soul is reborn into a different human personality. When that new personality at some future time enters the hereafter, whom does the soul represent? Also, can a soul have many reincarnations?

Why does God permit evil to exist? I truly wish I knew the answer to that question. If you accept the notion that hell does not exist in the afterlife, then evil must only exist on earth and dwell within the human mind. The first appearance of evil was in the garden of Eden, where the devil was represented as a serpent.

Can you really accept as factual the story about Adam and Eve in the garden of Eden, wherein Satan, disguised as a serpent, urged Adam to eat from the forbidden fruit,

CHAPTER 4

thus committing the first sin by disobeying the word of God. Think about that for a moment. A talking snake urging Adam to go against God? Who makes up these tales? Yes, yes, I get it! It is a story to get the point across not to disobey God. But why make it such a fairy tale? Doing so just turns many people away from a true and loving God.

Also, the Catholic Church holds that "all who die in God's grace and friendship but still imperfectly purified" undergo a process of purification. The church calls that purification process *purgatory*. The intent of purgatory is for the soul to achieve the holiness necessary to enter the joy of heaven."

The preceding quote is from a search on Google using the question "Where is purgatory in the Bible?"

Thus, as long as you are not in what is called mortal sin, your soul still will at some point enter God's heaven. This concept I can accept; however, to me, purgatory is a form of reincarnation. As I noted in chapter 4, a soul that has not earned entry to the afterlife may possibly get a do-over!

According to Roman Catholic theology, there are seven deadly (mortal) sins. They are pride, greed, lust, envy, gluttony, wrath, and sloth. While most humans are guilty of one or more of those, don't panic! The reason why you should not panic is that they can be forgiven by what is a confession to a priest. Also, while you may exhibit some of them, it doesn't mean you have committed a grave sin. The reason is it is very difficult to do so. The teaching of the religion is that to commit a mortal sin, three things must occur:

1. You *must* be aware that the action you are about to do is considered a grave mortal sin.
2. You *must* give considerable thought to the fact it is a mortal sin if you commit it.
3. You *actually* commit the act.

CHAPTER 4

If any one of the preceding is absent in that process, it is not considered a mortal sin. Now think about it! How many people go through that process? If you truly don't know the action you do is a mortal sin, it isn't! Also, if you knew it was a mortal sin and did not truly contemplate it, again, it is not a mortal sin. And finally, even if you know it is a mortal sin and you gave considerable thought to it, but you do not commit it, it is not a mortal sin. You see, it really is difficult to commit a mortal sin. It is noted in biblical teaching that Jesus, when he was on the cross, said out loud, "Father, forgive them for they do not know what they are doing!"

Having described what constitutes a grave sin, is it possible that what may not be a grave sin to one person is a grave sin to another person? Let's ponder that for a few seconds. Assume one person is taught and thus believes that a particular act is a grave sin, and another person was taught and believes the same act is not a grave sin. This is a dilemma for sure! According to the church teaching, regardless of the actual act, it would be a grave sin if the process described was indeed done. So, yes, the act for one person can be a grave sin while the same act for another person is not a grave sin.

I have often wondered if overzealous religious teachers are more responsible for grave sins being committed by people as a result of what they taught them. Is that possible? As I see it, it is!

CHAPTER 5

REINCARNATION

CHAPTER 5

While researching ADE stories, I discovered there appears to be creditable evidence of souls that have experienced previous human lives in a process known as reincarnation. Most of those events revolve around children under the age of five or six years old. It appears as the child grows older, the memory of a past life fades. In my attempt to rationalize the process of reincarnation and being educated in the science of engineering, I initially took an approach that was scientific in nature. Let me give you an example.

The mass of a living human body contains many different elements, such as hydrogen, oxygen, nitrogen, iron, selenium, potassium, and so on. When a human dies, over time, the body decomposes, and those elements are liberated and free to be absorbed by other life forms. Those life forms can be human, plant, or another type of living entity. As those elements may enter a different life form, can that be considered a form of reincarnation? Also, do any of those elements carry memory? I have given a lot of thought to this subject, and the conclusion I have arrived at is it does not meet the criteria for the true concept of reincarnation. The reason is reincarnation is not material; it is spiritual. It is the soul that must be incarnated, not the body. So, having come to that conclusion, it left me with more questions that I am not capable of rationalizing. Can it be the *do-over* of an unearned soul? I don't know; however, stories of reincarnation are quite compelling, and therefore, this chapter is devoted to that subject.

Some prominent religions of the world believe in and teach their followers about the concept of reincarnation. An example is in the teachings of Hinduism. The belief is that when one dies, the spirit or soul takes on a new body, and depending on the purity of the soul at the time of passing, the new body can be human, animal, or spiritual. In the Hindu religion, the soul gets a do-over until it rises to the level of spiritual.

CHAPTER 5

While there are different sects within Christianity, the principal tenet does not subscribe to the concept of reincarnation. The main belief is that the soul will remain dormant until Judgment Day when it will rise with a new body for the final judgment. While that is still the basic belief, there are elements within Christianity that are accepting of the concept of reincarnation. Also, if that belief is the only truth, there cannot be saints. Saints were humans who crossed the line of death and according to church teachings, must complete a number of miracles to be considered for sainthood. How can that be if the soul remains dormant? In any event, it is a popular belief as depicted by the following:

One of the most famous people in modern history who believed in reincarnation was General George Patton. He implied he had lived previous lives and recalled aspects of those lives. It is reported he believed he was a warrior back in Roman times and even experienced combat as a

Roman legionnaire. His beliefs were unshakable. When he was a young boy, he believed he fought Turkish armies. As he grew older, he continued to have visions of past deaths, even experiencing Viking funerals and recalling the battle of Tire. His past-life beliefs are well documented, and anyone who watched the movie Patton should be enlightened to that fact. While many people write off those comments by the general, his eerie stories are quite interesting. In most respects, the general was a traditional Christian and prayed often. The amazing aspect of the general's claim is that it is many lives he recalls, not just one.

A most noted and interesting reincarnation story is that of a four-year-old boy named Ryan. It is reported that Ryan holds many memories of a previous life. One such previous-life memory came to light when he played that he was the director of an imaginary movie. He would shout out, "Action!" whenever he would see a camera. At first, his parents didn't think much about it,

CHAPTER 5

but they became concerned after he started to wake up in the middle of the night claiming he had heart problems when he lived before in Hollywood. It appeared that Ryan couldn't let go of the feeling he lived in Hollywood. He told his mother that he believed he was someone else who lived there in the past and claimed he had three sons in his other life. He said they all lived in a large white house with a swimming pool. His mother become concerned, and after an exhausting investigation, she determined that his previous life may have been that of a man named Marty Martyn, a noted Hollywood agent. This is a well-documented case, and if you have interest in further understanding his claims, just type his name into the search engine on a computer. You will discover much interesting supporting information.

The following information is from an article on the website Graveyard Shift titled, "People with Really Believable Evidence for Their Claim They're Reincarnated" by Erin Wisti. I paraphrase in the following paragraphs.

A young girl from Sri Lanka named Purnima Ekanayake began speaking of a past life. After going on a school trip to a temple about 145 miles from her present home, she claimed that in another life she had lived in the town across the river from the temple they were at. In her past life, she said she was male and was an incense maker who died in a traffic accident. Ekanayake's father along with his brother-in-law decided to investigate her claim and traveled to that town. When there, they inquired about incense makers and learned of a man named Jinadasa who was killed by a bus while he was riding his bicycle. Ekanayake's family took Purnima to Jinadasa's home, where she was able to identify his wife and daughter and name the school Jinadasa attended. Prior to their meeting, there was no contact between those families. Other than reincarnation, it is difficult to explain how she knew such information.

Another interesting reincarnation story is that of a five-year-old boy by the name of Luke. Whenever Luke would

CHAPTER 5

play with his toys, he had the tendency to call them "Pam" and at first. I read that Luke's mother laughed it off. Luke told his mother that in his other life he was a girl and had black hair. Out of curiosity, his mother asked Luke who Pam was. Luke told his mother, "I was, but I died and went to heaven." He said he saw God. "Then God pushed me back down, and when I woke up, I was a baby, and you named me Luke." After she pressed him for more details, Luke told his mother in his other life he lived in Chicago, took the train a lot, and died in a fire. After mentioning his death, Luke made a hand motion indicating someone jumping out of a window. When his mother typed that information into a search engine on her computer, she discovered a news story that described a fire at a hotel in Chicago in 1993 where nineteen people died. One of them was a woman by the name of Pam Robinson, who died when she jumped out the hotel window.

There was no way his mother could explain how Luke knew of that fire or how Pam Robinson died. Luke had never been to Chicago, nor did anyone ever discuss anything like that with him.

What I found very interesting about this story is that it ties heaven and God together as part of the reincarnation process. Also, it appears that the soul has no specific gender. There are also other stories of reincarnation wherein the reincarnated claimed to be the opposite sex in a previous life experience.

A *Reader's Digest* story I read on the web described a two-year-old boy who said to his father, "When I was your age, I changed your diaper." Bewildered by this and other statements the boy made over the following months, his parents questioned him about why he was making those remarks. At that point, it became clear to them that the boy believed he was his grandfather in another life. Having come to that conclusion, they asked him, "Did you have any siblings?" The boy responded he had a sister "who turned into a fish." What is remarkable about that statement is that the boy's grandfather had had a sister who was discovered floating in the ocean, dead.

CHAPTER 5

A similar story is making the rounds on TikTok: "Reincarnation Is Real." I saw the video today on my computer. It is about a two-year-old girl who insists she is her great-great-grandmother. This came to light when the child saw her grandmother and great-great-grandmother together in a photograph, pointed to her great-great-grandmother, and said, "That's me!" Upon hearing that, the child's mother took her camera and started to film her daughter as she continued to say it. Apparently, there are hundreds of stories similar to this on the internet.

The following story was published by Wikipedia, and it is about a little girl by the name of Shanti Devi. Shanti was born in Delhi, India, on December 11, 1926, and died at the age of sixty-one on December 27, 1987. As a young girl of about four years of age, Shanti claimed she remembered a past life and was known by the name Lugdi Devi. She told her parents that her real home was in Mathura where her husband lived. She also shared several unique features about her husband. She said he had a fair complexion, wore glasses, and had a large wart on his left cheek, all of which turned out to be factual. In addition, she said her husband worked at his shop that was in front of the Dwarkadhish temple in Mathura. Her claim became the subject of reincarnation research, and a commission was set up by the Indian political leader Mahatma Gandhi, who supported her claim.

In reading many stories of reincarnated people, it is clear to me that the human soul has no specific gender. In one life, it may be associated to a human male and in another to a female. Can this be why some people identify themselves as being a sex other than what their current human form is? I don't have an answer to that question, but it is an interesting thought.

The following is a story I read on Facebook. It was written by Michelle Bee.

> So many years ago, my mum passed suddenly. She was at work and collapse of a brain hemorrhage. She was an RGN. It

CHAPTER 5

affected me really badly and I have never spoken about her death or even have picture up as I find it too distressing.

Six years later I had my first child and [her] first grandchildren. She was about 4 or 5 when she said mum I cannot wait to go to bed. I asked why? And she said because nannie Jue comes to see me.

Taken back as I couldn't figure out how she even knew her name—Judith. Not something I ever talk about and if I do I use "me mum."

Anyway, I thought for a bit and decided to question her. I was blown away. She said nanna Jue always holds her finger to my lip and says shhh. My mum always told me you have that dint under between your nose and lips because when you were a baby the angels come to say shhh.

She then told me my mum was the same height as me with short brown hair, with silver bits. (cos she was going grey). She wore a blue dress to her knees with green belt and a large silver buckle. (Her uniform was navy blue and she worn a nurse's belt). It too was navy blue but while training it was green. She said she wore earrings—small gold ones.

Oddly, I wasn't scared or frightened, athough I was upset and moved.

A week or so later I was visited by my brother and told him my daughter sees mum at night. He didn't believe me and gave me that look. So, I asked my daughter to tell him what she has told me. I asked the same questions…he started listening and saying how does she know that?

She kept looking to the right side of her. So, I asked is nannie Jue here now. She said

CHAPTER 5

yes but she has to go. Where does she have to go? I asked. Her reply absolutely blew me away and my brother who was sitting down shot up and almost ran out the room.

She has to go see her friend. Her friend is Ellen.

That was my mum's best friend while training. They had become estranged some years ago as they both followed different nursing paths and spare time was consumed with looking after relatives. I know at the time of mum's funeral, Ellen was unable to attend as she was caring for her brother with cancer.

I found this such an interesting story and another possible confirmation of reincarnation.

There are many people who subscribe to and believe in reincarnation—so many that there are a number of groups that research the subject. Those groups have a wealth of information regarding past lives and are willing to share the information with you. If your interest is in this field of study, you can find groups on the internet. One such site is Facebook. Don't be afraid to investigate them.

Chapter 6

Coins, Feathers, and Scents

CHAPTER 6

While the title of this chapter appears to be odd in a book about ADEs, there are many stories of the meaning of coins, feathers, and scents as they relate to the departed. Therefore, I would be remiss if I did not describe some of those meanings.

Many people believe finding coins and feathers and experiencing scents are significant as they relate to the departed. For example, finding coins after a loved one dies is said to have the following meanings:

Penny

Finding a penny, particularly in the heads-up position, is a reminder of God! On the head side of a penny are the words "In God We Trust." Also, finding a penny is thought to be significant in that some believe it was put there by an angel who was crossing your path. The old saying goes "Pennies from heaven." Many people also believe it is meant to bring comfort and love from a departed one. Finding a single penny signifies you are still connected to a loved one in the spirit world. Finding two or three pennies together has a different significance. There are many meanings of finding a penny, most influenced by culture.

CHAPTER 6

Nickel

When you find a nickel on the ground, many believe that to be a sign from the spiritual realm not to carry the burden of a departed loved one but to live life more freely and to take more risks. It is said that the mere fact that the nickel is in your path is a divine omen of support from the departed loved one

Dimes

This one is my favorite, perhaps because recently I found two dimes each a day apart. The saying goes that if you find a dime, it implies that a loved one who died wants you to know they are looking out for you. That sure sounds like my beloved wife. When alive, she always looked out for and took good care of me.

I read stories of people who claimed that they would find coins in their home even after they cleaned the house. That is, they cleaned a particular room where there were no coins, only to reenter the room at a later time and discover the coin or coins in plain sight. I found their stories a bit eerie. The fact is they are very sincere in citing them.

Feathers

Finding feathers also is said to have a significant connection to the departed. Many claim that finding an all-white feather implies it is a form of communication from a deceased loved one. It is also believed to be a message from an angel of love and encouragement.

Finding a gray feather has the meaning that a period of calm and clarity is about to enter your life.

Scents

There are many reports that from time to time people smell the scent of a loved one who is in the after world. What does it mean when this occurs? Some believe that a loved one in the afterlife is contacting you in a nonscary way to let you know they are looking in on you and that they are still around. In my research thus far, I have not determined where this belief originated. In any event, it is a comforting thought.

CHAPTER 6

In addition to coins, feathers, and scents that essentially apply to the living world, the following are some colors and plants that many of those who died and returned to life so vividly describe seeing while in the afterlife.

There are a number of stories in which a person who died and returned to life described how while being in the afterlife they found themselves in a wonderful field filled with strange trees, plants, and flowers in colors they never saw before. This description is not singular but told by many. Therefore, illusion by drugs or mindset must be discounted. Since many people have described similar experiences, it should be taken seriously.

To emphasize the recalling of strange colors and flowers, I cite from Jeremey Well's ADE story:

"I saw fields of different types of flowers they were all different colors, beautiful colors I have never seen before on earth."

Also, Jim, in his ADE story, said that he saw beautiful flowers of different colors.

There are many others that can be cited. If you are still doubting there is an afterlife, how do you explain that so many ADE stores are so similar to each other in terms of what they experienced?

Chapter 7

Statements of an Afterlife

CHAPTER 7

This chapter lists various statements made by people who believe in an afterlife and related such publicly.

The following was written by Yassimine A. E. I paraphrase,

> My husband who is atheist "which is perfectly fine with me", holds a PHD in philosophy and man he is toooo rational, he did not believe in anything that is not logical or scientific. After our cat Biscuit died in his arms, in his office, he had a visit from her the next day. She pulled the covers on him; he was lying in the bed he sleeps in sometimes in his office when he has a lot of work to do. He saw the covers being pulled over him as if by an invisible hand, he panicked, but instantly a tiny paw patted his shoulder! He knew it was Biscuit! He was

not asleep; he was still awake. He also saw dreams where she [w]as in a very nice place with fantastic garden.

Lately he is seeing people he had not seen in years few minutes after he thinks of them. Or he sees them in dreams and the next morning he runs into them! My husband is very kind and self-denying and I am glad that this is happening to him to reassure both of us and give us hope, the kind of hope I was desperate to find. I wanted to share this with you to convey the same hope to anyone who might be in need for it.

I mention the religious beliefs of my husband cuz it means a lot when this testimony comes from someone who did not have such beliefs, when it comes from believers,

CHAPTER 7

it could be perceived as biased or wishful thinking or affected by one's ideologies.

Peace xx.

Wow! What a testimony! An atheist becoming a believer! It sure sounds like animals do have souls.

Another story was written by Sherrie-Rich Tottleben H.:

My father-in-law passed away February 10, 1984. He had been in the hospital and in a coma for some time. It was my turn to sit with him the night before he passed away. Sometime during the late night, this man who had been in a coma for days, sat straight up in bed, looked at the door, smiled and said, "Awe Maude, I haven't seen you in so long!" I looked at the door because Maude, his sister passed away in 1975, the year before I met my husband. Of course, I didn't see anything. He lay back down, and I never heard another word out of him. When the family came in that morning around 8:00 am I told them Dad was going to die today because Maude was there to get him. They

CHAPTER 7

all thought I was nuts. Dad died at 8:36 am and I know in my heart Maude was there to take him home. I still get goose bumps to this day. I know there is an afterlife, and our loved ones will come get us to take us home. What a blessed day that will be.

What a wonderful experience that must have been for Sherrie-Rich! It is so beautiful and comforting to sense we are not alone when we cross over.

The following is a story I read on Facebook written by Robin Noyes.

Back in the day I used to skydive. I made a best friend there who was a nurse and we used to talk a lot about her job. She told me a story I would really like to share.

She worked in a hospital in the ER. One day they brought in a woman who had coded. She was dead. My friend was on staff that day and they had called everyone there who was on hand, to work on her, to get her "stable." They had done everything they could do but she had died. They still worked on her. Eventually, they got a heartbeat, and she came back. This went on and off though, as the woman kept dying. Eventually they did get her back and stable.

CHAPTER 7

They had admitted her with a chronic heart condition that they knew that later she would need surgery.

Fast forward one year. One year later this woman, who was thriving came back to the hospital. She wanted to thank everyone who had worked on her and done their best to save her life.

But there was more. There was one thing that had been bothering her for that entire year, so she had to go back. She had said when she was dead, she saw the entire medical team working on her—up above them. She was up above them all—in the room, but the ONE thing that bothered her was the fact that she saw something.

She had to come back to see.

She had told them that she saw three safety pins on top of the dusty top of the lights in the ER. She wanted to know if that was the case as she had seen them. It did not take long for someone to get a ladder to go up and see…

And there were three safety pins!

CHAPTER 7

The following story was written by Elaine Macdonald on Facebook. It is a story about reincarnation.

My daughter and I went to a museum/mill in Wales. On the road down to the mill my grandson, who was about 4, said that he had been there before. He remembered the road we were walking down. He asked if we were going to a mill where they made flour. When we got there, he said that the wheels were different…he didn't remember them like that. When we asked a member of staff about it, she said that the wheels were different, they get changed about every 100 years.

We went out to cross the bridge to have a look at the castle, but my grandson refused to move. He wouldn't walk on the bridge at all and burst into tears and said there were bad men there. So, we went back to speak to the lady in the museum about that and she said there had been a battle on the bridge many years previously.

Wow! A possible confirmation of reincarnation told by the boy's grandmother.

CHAPTER 7

The following story is by Kelly Jo Meeks and was noted on Facebook:

> I'm a nurse now but at the time I was a CAN and had the honor of caring for a beautiful young man with down syndrome. He had been diagnosed with a brain tumor and was given 6 months to live but was going on 6 years when I was assigned to his case. I would go to his home everyday to bathe him. He fell ill one day shortly after I left from giving his bath and was hospitalized with severe pneumonia and sepsis. After a few days, I had some time off and I decided to sit with his mom at the hospital, so she wasn't alone and she made the hard decision to let him go. We sat with him each holding a hand, while we talked ad kept each other

company. At one point she got up to go to the bathroom and I suddenly felt a strong presence in the room, in the corner stood 3 men, they looked like monks in brown cloaks strangely, hoods and all, I couldn't see their faces, they didn't speak but I knew they were there to get him. I quietly said, "I'm not ready to let go" and before I could finish the sentence they were gone. I didn't tell his mom what happened because I was really trying to process it myself. I can't remember how much time passed but his mom went into the hallway a little later to speak to the nurse and the monks were back, this time they spoke but not audibly I heard them in my head if that makes any sense and they said, "this time we have to take him with us when we go." His mom

CHAPTER 7

returned and we continued to sit on each side of his bed holding his hand, a few minutes went by, and he woke up looked across the room, smiled real big and closed his eyes again, he hadn't been conscious for a few days at that point so we were surprised, within a few minutes he took his last breath and was gone. Seeing that smile on his face I knew that he saw what I saw, and they took him with them this time just like they said they would. It gave me peace and 20 years later when I think about it its just as clear as it was that day. I have more experiences I'll share with you as well. Be blessed!

This is such a beautiful story, and it reminded me of what my niece told me her mother saw just prior to her crossover.

Chapter 8

Provocative Thoughts

CHAPTER 8

As the heading implies, the contents of this chapter include and offer the reader provocative thoughts regarding religion, God, prayer, and the afterlife.

Provocative Thought 1

Have you ever wondered why God is always referred to as masculine? It is the Father, the Son, and the Holy Spirit (also referred to as the Holy Ghost). We know that the terms *father* and *son* depict masculine gender, but few reference the Holy Spirit's gender. Can it be because it was *man* who wrote the scripture?

There is no doubt that in most religions of the world, including Christianity (according to Wikipedia the largest with 2.8 billion followers), females are considered second-class entities. An example of that is in the Catholic religion and evident when the ritual of baptism is performed. If there is more than one child being baptized, the males are always baptized first. The females are always baptized last. Also, in the Catholic Church, women cannot be ordained as priests. Why is that? Are females not equal to males in the eyes of God? Is that really possible? Of course not! When there is a father, mother, and child, the traditional family is complete. The provocative

CHAPTER 8

thought here is that the Holy Spirit is the feminine quality of the Holy Trinity, and God consists of three divine personalities and a duality in gender.

I am not alone in that belief, and in support of that thought, the following paragraph is from the Saint Cecilia Catholic Community website (saintceciliacatholiccommunity.org).

The Holy Trinity is like a family, the Family of God, the Father, the Son and Holy Spirit. But a biological family is not possible without a father and mother. So, even though the Holy Spirit is not named Mother, the Holy Spirit possesses the characteristics of Divine Motherhood as the Father possesses those of Divine Fatherhood. The Holy Spirit's activities are expressed in "giving birth" "nurturing" "forming" and "mothering" all the Father's creation. Also, in Hebrew, the grammatical gender for the word *spirit* (*Ruach*) denotes feminine qualities.

In the Aramaic language, the language generally thought of as that spoken by Jesus, the word for spirit is feminine.

Provocative Thought 2

This particular provocation deals with gender identity. We all know people who live their lives as the opposite sex to what they physically are. Why is that? Can it be that in a previous life they indeed may have been? There are many reports wherein reincarnated children relate that possibility. While there are many reports, two are noted in chapter 5 in the reincarnated stories of Purnima Ekanayake and Luke. They both describe how in previous lives they were the opposite sex than they currently are experiencing. From those accounts, it appears that the soul must be gender neutral. If that is truly the case, then those who live their current lives as being other than their current sex are quite possibly not necessarily wrong in the eyes of God.

CHAPTER 8

Provocative Thought 3

This provocation is to challenge certain words in The Lord's Prayer that should be deleted. Those words are "Lead us not into temptation." Why are those words there? God the Father is all about love. It is inconceivable the Father would lead anyone into temptation that can lead to sin.

Provocative Thought 4

This particular provocation deals with the possibility that all living entities are blessed with a soul. The basis of this thought is the fact animals have the ability to think. We also know they can learn and have memory. Why is it then many people assume they don't have a soul? Like human life, animal life is energy, and energy cannot be destroyed; it can only change form.

In support of this provocation, there are reports by some people who experienced ADEs that they were met by past pets in the afterlife. How did the pets get there if it were not their soul?

CHAPTER 8

Provocative Thought 5

Is there such a thing as a lost soul? It appears that the human body is not an eternal thing, but instead, the soul is. It is the soul that has an afterlife, not the body. In support of this thought, I suggest that if reincarnation is real, and there is evidence to support that theory, then the soul is shepherd to the body and is the entity that has eternal life.

Provocative Thought 6

At one time, I believed in extraterrestrials (ETs). I don't anymore. However, let's assume there is life on planets other than earth. Do they worship the same God, and is there a Jesus-like figure there also?

Is God god of the universe or only of earth's solar system? This provocative thought can only be individualized. I personally believe there is one God, and thus, should ETs arrive on earth in the future, they must believe in the same God I do. What do you think?

About the Author

After military service Gerard J. De Santis earned a Mechanical Engineering Degree from Fairleigh Dickinson University. He is the author of a number of technical papers on pumps and hydraulic systems and is the author of two books. PUMP-NOLOGY and COLD WAR VETERAN'S HONOR.